Curandera

Books by Carmen Tafolla:

Poetry:

Get Your Tortillas Together

Curandera

Sonnets to Human Beings & Other Selected Works

Sonnets to Human Beings/ Sonnette an menschen

Sonnets and Salsa

Rebozos

Fiction:

The Holy Tortilla and a Pot of Beans

Non-Fiction:

To Split a Human: Mitos, Machos y la Mujer Chicana

Recognizing the Silent Monster: Racism in the 90s

Tamales, Comadres, & the Meaning of Civilization

A Life Crossing Borders: Memoir of a Mexican-American Confederate / Las memorias de un mexicoamericano en la Confederacion

For Children:

Baby Coyote and the Old Woman / El coyotito y la viejita

That's Not Fair! Emma Tenayuca's Struggle for Justice / ¡No Es Justo! La lucha de Emma Tenayuca por la justicia

The Dog Who Wanted to Be a Tiger

What Can You DO With a Rebozo?

What Can You DO With a Paleta?

Fiesta Babies

Carmen Tafolla

Thirtieth Anniversary Edition

With a new introduction by
Norma Elia Cantú

Prólogo original por Rolando Hinojosa

Illustrations by Thelma Ortíz Muraida

WingsPress

San Antonio, Tejas
2012

Curandera © 1983, 1987, 2012 by Carmen Tafolla.
Curandera was first published by M&A Editions (San Antonio, Tejas)
in 1983. A second edition was published by Santa Monica College Press /
Lalo Press (La Jolla, CA) in 1987.
Cover and internal art © 1983, 1987, 2012 by Thelma Ortiz Muraida.
Photographs provided by Carmen Tafolla, Bryce Milligan
and Moisés Sandoval.
Prólogo © 1983 by Rolando Hinojosa.

Thirtieth Anniversary Edition

Print Edition ISBN: 978-1-60940-237-2

Ebook ISBN: 978-1-60940-240-2

Wings Press

On-line catalogue and ordering:
www.wingspress.com
All Wings Press titles are distributed to the trade by
Independent Publishers Group
www.ipgbook.com

Al Sol De Mi Vida

CONTENTS

I. POEMAS CASEROS

II. SPIRITS BETWEEN SIGLOS

III. CUENTOS PARA EL CURANDERO

IV. UN TECITO

Cecilio García-Camarillo, Reyes Cárdenas, and Carmen Tafolla.
West Side, San Antonio, Tejas, 1975.
Photograph by César Martínez.

Ernesto Bernal, Mari, Carmen Tafolla and Alex Haley (1985).

Introduction:
A blessing and an abrecaminos
para Carmen Tafolla y su *Curandera*

Curandera. Healer. Shaman. She who brings succor. She who brings life. She who brings comfort. She who keeps the sacred medicine. She who knows. She who writes. Curandera. Healer. Shaman.

I introduce Carmen Tafolla's *Curandera* with deep gratitude for the honor of writing about a book that touched my heart all those years ago. I'd like to begin with a brief history of the poemario's publication and then write about the poems themselves, all of this interwoven with my own memories of the poetry and the book. Not surprising, given the way our literature was published back then, *Curandera* took a while to be birthed. Several years in fact. Tafolla tells me she'd been writing the poems as individual poems; she was not thinking of a collection or of any particular theme until half the poems were written. Once those were assembled, the collection came together nicely, almost magically, and it became clear that it was becoming *Curandera*. She ordered the book into four sections: *Poemas Caseros, Spirits Between Siglos, Cuentos para el Curandero, and Un Tecito*.

When the late Jim Cody of Place of Herons Press showed an interest, she gave him the collection she called *Curandera*. It was the late 70s. Times were hard. Jim kept the manuscript for a couple of years, and due to financial constraints of the 70s economic crisis (seems we have one every decade), informed Tafolla that it would probably be another two or three years before the press could afford to print the book so he was releasing the manuscript; she was free to find another publisher.

Serendipitously, Chicana poet and activist Angela de Hoyos, que en paz descanse, and her husband Moisés were looking for poetry to publish in their Chicano press, M&A Editions. According to Tafolla, Angela told her, "We want to publish a book of your poems." Tafolla immediately thought of the "librito" that Jim had just released. Sure, I have a collection you can publish, she answered. It took another year before it was published, but finally *Curandera* existed in this world as a book of poems.

An Offering. A Medicine Bag. A collection of words that heal and instruct. A librito with its own history, its own story.

Curandera

M&A editions in 1983 was a collaborative labor of love, as the author's acknowledgments attest. As they prepared the manuscript for publication, Tafolla looked around for someone to introduce the book; she asked Rolando Hinojosa, at the time one of the very few Chicano literary critics. He readily agreed. His words resonate even now with the deep respect for the poet

Angela De Hoyos, publisher and editor of M&A Editions and Huehuetitlan, *and Susana de la Torre, editor of* Caracol. *Early 1970s.*

he talks of and the pitfalls that Tafolla avoids in presenting her personal but universal view of San Antonio, indeed of what could've been any Chicano barrio of the time. San Antonio artist Thelma Ortíz Muraida, with whom Tafolla had collaborated before on a series of poster poems, agreed to illustrate the book. She designed the cover, and drew from the poems and from her own reality to create the drawings for each of the sections. The woman behind the screen door is her own abuelita. Thanks to

Back row: Angela De Hoyos and Moisés Sandoval (publisher and printer, respectively, of M&A Editions), novelist Max Martínez, future scholar Yolanda Broyles-González, and artist Ramón Vasquez y Sánchez. Front row: poet José "Black Hat" Montalvo, musician and poet Juan Tejeda, and poet Raúl Salinas. San Antonio, Texas, ca. 1978.

Sister Dorothy Folliard, *Curandera* was presented to the public at the Mexican American Cultural Center in San Antonio. Tafolla remembers that it was well attended and that Frank Pino "presented" the book with a few words. The event included an exhibit of Muraida's art work for the book. Immediately it became part of Chicana/o literary history as it was disseminated throughout the Southwest: California, Texas, New Mexico, Arizona.

Not too long after that, Ernesto Padilla and Yolanda Luera who ran Lalo Press based in Santa Monica, California, published a second edition (1987) and a third edition (1993). The bright turquoise blue with the distinctive hand lettering of the title and the art work attracts and impels a reader to open it, to delve into its healing woman wisdom. The Alex Haley blurb always intrigued me. How did Haley come to write the blurb? Well, as in most cases, there's a story there, too. Tafolla offered it to Haley as a regalito at a function in California where he was presenting a speech in 1984. He called her the next day to tell her that he had read it straight through that night and was coming back to Fresno in two weeks—could they meet? Over enchiladas at Tafolla's home, he told her how much it had echoed, for him, the poetry of Africaniste poets he had heard read in Paris recently, and offered her the blurb, to be used in the next edition.

This is more than an introduction; it is a critical review, a meditation on what this librito means to me and to Chicana/o literature, indeed to the larger canon of U.S. literary production.

In those early days, it was not easy to find works by women writers, especially Chicanas. I know because I was always looking for material for my classes. Tafolla's librito was a treasure! I bought it from Juan Rodriguez who with his wife of the time, Petra, owned Relámpago Books, a book distribution business along with a very small publishing set up.

They rendered an invaluable service to writers and readers of Chicana/o literature. Being in Laredo, Texas, it was especially hard for me to find books published by small Chicano presses. Relámpago was a godsend. My path didn't intersect with Tafolla's in the 70s since I was in Nebraska pursuing my doctorate degree. I returned to Texas in 1980. Alas, we didn't meet then. I believe it was Angela de Hoyos who first mentioned her to me. Tafolla had just left Texas for California in late 1983, a month after the publication of *Curandera*. But her poems appeared in *Huehuetitlán*, the literary publication that Angela and Moisés put together periodically and where many Tejana and Tejano writers first published. M&A constituted an oasis for writers in Tejas. As Tafolla soon found out when she moved to California, Chicanas were erased, excluded, everywhere. She tells me with sadness in her voice, "When I applied at CSUF (California State University, Fresno) for a tenure track faculty position in Women's Studies in 1984, just months after *Curandera* was released, and after the *To Split a Human: Mitos, Machos y La Mujer Chicana* book had been published by MACC, the all-white search committee actually asked

*Carmen Tafolla (left) at a predominantly male
Chicano Studies conference in 1975.*

me, 'Yes, we see you have many publications about Chicana women, but do you have anything that's about WOMEN?'"

As Tafolla has done time and again, she became a trailblazer, and was hired as Associate Professor, the first tenure-track faculty person in Women's Studies at Cal State Fresno. But all the while, *Curandera* was opening a path for Tafolla as it gained popularity and readers kept asking for more.

I remember reading *Curandera* and going back to it time and again. It possessed a power that moved me, reminded me of that one poem I read in a Chicano literary *revista* in the stacks at the Texas A&I University library one Saturday afternoon in the fall of 1974; it impacted me so strongly that to this day tears well up when I think of it. It was a poem about picking cotton that struck a chord and that taught me that I too could write about such things. It was a veritable epiphany. In similar fashion, reading Tafolla's *Curandera* unlocked doors and allowed me to walk right into the world of Chicana poetry that blended folklore and traditional folklife, all told in Spanglish!

A few years ago, a doctoral student was doing a Directed Reading with me on Tejana poetry and bemoaned the fact that so many of our poets have gone unrecognized. We commiserated about the erasure of so many poets whose *libritos* are out of print, or who published in journals that are long gone and are therefore inaccessible to contemporary readers. We vowed to someday put together an anthology to bring these forgotten poems to new readers. Tafolla's *Curandera* was on the top of my list. "A century of Tejana poetry" would be our subtitle. For now that project remains a dream, but I am certain that it will see the light some day.

Tafolla's *Curandera* has been out of print for two decades. When a friend of mine, Prof. Maria Henríquez Betancort, from the Universidad de la Laguna in Las Palmas, a scholar of Chicana literature asked if I knew how to get a copy of the book for a project she was working on, I called Tafolla and asked if she had any copies of the book. She told me that she had some "*curandera* innards"—the unbound pages of 40 copies—which she had been toting around from place to place: California, Arizona, el Valle in South Texas, and of course, San Antonio. We concocted a plan and approached Bryce Milligan at Wings Press, who agreed to hand bind those original sheets into a special limited edition to accompany the publication of this 30th anniversary edition. That is how such things happen, de pura chiripada. One thing leads to another. Serendipity. Pure and simple. And voilà, here we are. We are now part of *Curandera's* publishing history.

What do you want readers to get out of this book? I ask Tafolla. "The same thing I did when it was first published," she answers. "I want them to appreciate their own internal strength. To know that socioeconomic status does not define the extent of their potential. I want them to get in touch with their spiritual power. To appreciate the beauty of our culture, of our traditions."

The Poetry

The power of the words in *Curandera* transcends the page and reaches into the heart. On several levels it is part of a long legacy of poetic form in Chicana/o community, the oral tradition, the oral recitation of poetry, declamación, and serves as a precursor of many poets who would come much later, "spoken word" poets like Tammy Gómez, slam poets like Jessica Helen López. At the time Tafolla was writing the poems that would later appear in *Curandera*, Chicano poetry was mostly male dominated; those who wrote of the pachuco like José Montoya and the pinto poets like Raul Salinas and Ricardo Sánchez were celebrated. Luis Omar Salinas, Reyes Cárdenas. It was such a patriarchal world, Tafolla reminds me, that one of her stories that was published in *Festival Flor y Canto II: An Anthology of Chicano Literature* was attributed to a male writer. As things went back then, the event happened in March 1975 but the anthology was not published until 1979. Tafolla was very pleased that the editors took her cuentos and poems, of course, but dismayed to see that due to their assigning the wrong authorship to her story, all the short stories published appeared to have been written by males. That was such a different time period, and presses and universities were not very open to Chicano literature, even less so to Chicana Literature or to poetry. Even within Chicano Literary circles, the icons were forming around Pachucos and male migrant worker stories, NEVER around women. So, I heralded the voice in *Curandera.* According to Tafolla, her poem "Los Corts 3 (la pachuquita)" may have been the first time a young pachuca appeared in the literature; it was written in 1975 and performed that same year, even before Inés Hernández' "tough girl" poem "To Teresa" appeared. We were all very aware at that point that the males were focusing only on a male world. Tafolla remembers questioning this state of affairs: "but *my* experience of Chicano Culture had two genders in it, sometimes three." What she wanted was to inscribe las mujeres into that Chicano world that the males were portraying where they didn't exist, or if they did, they absolutely had no agency and remained silent shadows. She says, "I wanted to focus on la pachuquita, la viejita, la madre, la curandera, la rebelde, on full, living, breathing females."

This lyrical poetry, rife with "right on" Spanglish, quickly became a favorite source to go to for examples of the use of folklore ("Curandera" and Caminitos"), of powerful women ("Tía Sofía" and "Curandera"), and of the land ("Cuilmas" and "Pozo Libre"). Before terms like flash fiction or ecofeminism were in common use, examples of these could be found in this collection.

Curandera opens the path for many other poets. It precedes Gloria Anzaldua's use of Chicana/o Spanish, and while it is a product of its time, and may strike contemporary readers as too safe and not political, it was anything but safe at its time, as an indictment of the historical racist world of the barrios in Texas and throughout the Southwest, even as it celebrates the culture and the people who inhabit these spaces.

The book is divided into four parts, *Poemas Caseras, Spirits Between Siglos, Cuentos para el Curandero* and *Un Tecito.* I remember marveling at the "wrong" usage of "Poemas caseras." When *This Bridge Called my Back* was translated as "Esta Puente mi espalda," I remembered the Chicano Spanish with its idiosyncratic gender agreement. After several trips to Spain and Mexico, where they, too, found *Curandera* relevant, Tafolla changed the phrase to the more universal "Poemas Caseros." Tafolla begins "Poemas Caseros" with an elegy to her aunt who "speaks Tex-Mex/with Black English, and all the latest slang." This is followed by a piece of what would now be called "flash fiction," a prose poem, a perfect example of what Tafolla does best, weave a tight narrative that surprises and shifts from past to present, pivoting on a line and bringing the reader to the poet's own rumination. She ends the poem about the old man who was always wanting to "go home" and the daughter who chides him with "Esa casa ya no existe," by inserting herself into the cycle, the rhythm of life: "Y a veces me siento cansada de trabajar y digo 'Ya me voy pa' la casa.' Y me siento a pensar, y me acuerdo...que esa casa ya no existe."

"Los Corts (5 voces)" is really five character sketches, short poems that Tafolla would perform transforming herself into the characters: the mother, the young boy, the teenage Pachuca, the dropout, the old woman. In "Los Corts 1 (la madre)," a welfare mother with an infant son and an older daughter speaks totally in Spanish of the oppressive heat of two o'clock in the afternoon, a metaphor for her constricted life; in "Los Corts 2 (el chamaquito)," a young boy eloquent in slang Spanish with a lexicon rooted in South Texas has found a dime, "un daime," and is planning to buy either "beisbol carts" or "dientes de wax." He will show that old woman who owns the shop, "que siempre me tá regañando," as he ends his dramatic monologue: "Pa que vea/ Pa que vea...." "Los Corts 3 (la pachuquita)" has La Dot as the protagonist who in typical teenage fashion tells a story, a quick code-switching snapshot of a typical high school exchange among young girls—she is defiant and exhibits a strong and determined stance in the face of a possible attack by La Silvia and her group. "¡You bet, muchacha! Aquí toy–lista!" She is the precursor of the gang members in the Allison Anders film, *Mi Vida Loca* and so many other teenage Chicanas who have been absent from Chicana literature. "Los Corts 4 (the dropout)" subtly indicts the schools for pushing Chicanos out, the speaker repeats, "Yo no *soy* tonto" and ends with a direct reference to the school's English-Only policy: "(And I wasn't spikking Spenish. I *wasn't!!)*" In the final poem, "Los Corts 5 (la viejita)," the old woman welcomes someone who presumably comes from the Church, for she works with El Padre Rodriguez: "Sí, entre, entre" and proceeds to reveal a life full of grief and of hardship with a Vietnam vet son, Rudy—Rodolfo like the woman's brother—who is bitter over the injustices he encounters, who seeks a job unsuccessfully, gets into fights, and sinks into depression. Her daughter Lupita is married and even Lupita's son has married, and the old woman's youngest granddaughter is already seven. In the prose poem Tafolla depicts the full life of the elderly widow who keeps her anger inside and private, but very strong, as she resists in alternate ways. "Aquí/adentrito,/y no le digo a nadien." The five poems are a prism through which the life of the barrio can be read. I agree with Rolando Hinojosa who writes in the introduction, "pone la mano en la llaga para hacer memoria de un dolor fuerte y nada agrio."

Part two, titled "Spirits between Siglos," explores in a more conventional poetic form the terrain around San Antonio, both its indigenous past and the contemporary Chicano landscape. The six poems shine like pebbles on the "Caminitos"—the pathways along the Medina River—as the poet explores the meaning of the spaces and of the past. "Cuilmas" (an old Chicano nickname for San Antonio, popularized with the pachucos of the 1940s, the footnote tells us) alludes to the "city's Spanish soul/Indian goal/Mexican music/and the cool whisper of the/Chicano/ 'cuilmas...'." In "Ancient House," the poet confronts herself and her mortality. Similarly in "Aquí" and in "¡Ajay!" she celebrates a man who lives a life filled with indigenous joy, but oblivious to his indigenous roots. It is here that we see how the poems are healing concoctions of the curandera, the healing woman who can cure a "Resfrío de alma." Tafolla introduces the short poem with a familiar lullaby "Rru-rru-rru" and a grandmother who tucks you in and prepares a tea awaiting relief for the cold that has gripped the soul.

In section three, "Cuentos Para el Curandero" we find the poet digging into old wounds. Three of the four poems in the section are lengthy explorations of racist and oppressive conditions. "Quality literature" has a World Literature professor refusing to consider a student's request to use Chicano literature for an assignment. "And When I Dream Dreams..." goes back to Rhodes Jr. School, "the toughest junior high in town," and reflects on the dire conditions where we meet an Air Force recruit seeking the GI Bill for a college education, Marcelino, who comes back a paraplegic from Vietnam, Sylvia who at age 15, waits tables and carries her second pregnancy, and Lalo and Lupe—all are signifiers for the school's failure to educate, to do its job. The poet graduated, survived, displays her B.A., M.A., Ph.D. and still dreams dreams of Rhodes Junior School.

The final section, "Un Tecito," begins with the powerful "Medicine Poem," a calling for a healing, for an end to war, an end to sickness. Centered on sickness that "lies around us like rotting feelings," that "nabs young black children playing in Atlanta," that "leaves health hiding in a grass roofed shack/in a Kickapoo Indian Village." The poem ends on a positive note proclaiming:

Our hurting, healing must run in the right direction
and swiftly, with quick glances back,
carrying with it always the medicine pouch, intact
with human bonding.
Must run, must heal, must leave behind
For wars
and poems
must always
have an end.

"Tierra Brujo" and "Rain Seeds" also sing a song of defiance or survival and of hope. In the former, we read that "por mas que han tratado/ nunca te han conquistado" and thus the land remains unconquered. And in the latter we read that rain seeds are "like drops of hope." That "await the time/to sprout."

The title poem, "Curandera," finds the poet outside the healer's home "entre la hierba buena y el anís" seeking and finding solace. But soon, the healer is in the poet's mind and body, and the leaves of her dreams are steeped in the healer's teapot.

The book ends with the love poem, "Y cuando pienso en tí," with the evocative phrase, un eterno querer. That is what *Curandera* ultimately becomes: a love song, for the healing occurs with love and a reclaiming of what is to be loved, the land, the traditions, all that an English-only, power-hungry, greedy world would destroy.

In this edition, Carmen Tafolla's *Curandera* comes back to life after 30 years, and no doubt it will find a home in many a Chicana or Chicano heart. Allow the poems to speak to you as they will, in Spanish, in English and in Spanglish sprinkled with Caló. Allow the tenderness and the healing energy of the words to carry you into that place of dreams where poems live, where poets take refuge. Carmen Tafolla's *Curandera* is magic and wonder. Allow it to awe you.

Curandera. Woman healer. Shaman. Hechizera. Granicera. She who heals. She who loves.

Norma Elia Cantú
San Anto, Tejas
February 6, 2012

CARACOL FOOD RAISER

Caracol fundraiser, ca. 1977. From left: José Reyna, Carmen Tafolla, Reyes Cárdenas, Max Martínez, Cecilio García-Camarillo, Mía García-Camarillo, Juan Tejeda, Susana de la Torre, Alfredo de la Torre, Angela De Hoyos, Evangelina (Vangie) Vigil.

Carmen Tafolla, 1983

Prólogo

Sabido es que hay gente por allí que indébidamente se apropia de la poesía como terapia personal, como desahogo estridente y sinrazón, y para el colmo de las cosas, como alarde tan hermético como insubstancial. En el caso de Carmen Tafolla, no hay nada de lo susodicho; certitud, claridad, y celebración de la vida es lo que se verá en esta retrospectiva de varios años de actividad poética.

Tafolla sabe quién es y de dónde viene; conoce y aprecia sus raíces méxico-texanas, maneja que no manipula el idioma, y lo encaja donde cabe y debe. Parece cosa fácil pero no lo es.

Segura de sí misma, esta poeta no sólo habla de sufrimiento y regocijo sino que también nos deja saber el dolor y el gozo a primera mano. Para comprobar, uno sólo tiene que leer *Tía Sofía, ancient house, and when I dream dreams...* y la joyita *Voyage*. También se verán recuerdos y reminiscencias como en *Los Corts* y en *Caminitos*, así como el uso de una prosa fuerte, de una prosa poética, pues. Y, todo con certeza y fibra, con el ojo claro y despejado que no se deja engañar por el sentimentalismo o por el pariente nocivo de éste, el romanticismo huero que tanto perjudica al sentimiento y a la razón.

Esto de escribir introducciones es oficio tan dudoso como incierto. A veces también es oficio poco respetable. De mi parte, le agradezco a Tafolla el tiempo que me dio para saborear, para gozar, y para reflexionar de lo que, en muy gran parte, se trata la vida.

Una nota más. El libro de poesía *Curandera* (así como el poema del mismo título) le encaja bien a Tafolla; pone la mano en la llaga para hacer memoria de un dolor fuerte y nada agrio. También lo hace para contar muchas verdades. Más, creo yo, no se le puede pedir al poeta.

Rolando Hinojosa
Austin, Texas
Mayo, 1983

I. Poemas Caseros

Tía Sofía

Mi Tía Sofía
sang the blues
at "A" Record Shop,
on the west side of downtown,
across from Solo-Serve's
Thursday coupon specials
she never missed.
  "Cuantro yardas de floral print cottons
  por solo eighty-nine cents—fíjate nomás, Sara,
  you'll never get it at that price anywhere else!"
  she says to her younger sister.
And "A" Record Shop
grows up the walls around her like vines
like the flowers and weeds and everything in her
green-thumb garden.
Here—
instead of cilantro and rosas
and Principe Dormido—
it's a hundred odd and only 45's
10 years too late
that'll never be sold
even after she dies
and a dozen hit albums that crawl up the wall,
smiling cool pachuco-young Sonny and the Sunglo's,
The Latin Breed, Flaco Jimenez, Toby Torres,
and the Royal Jesters.
Also: Little Stevie Wonder.
And The Supremes.
She sings to pass the time
"Ah foun' mah thr*ee*-uhl
own Blueberry H*ee*-uhl."

She also likes "Lavender Blue"
It seems to be her color,
but *bright*—in a big-flowered cotton print
(from Solo-Serve.)

Tía Sofía speaks Tex-Mex
with Black English,
and *all* the latest slang.
Not like the other aunts—
Tía Ester, always at home,
> haciendo caldo,
> haciendo guiso,
> haciendo tortillas,
> she never left the house
> except to go to church,
> braided her hair on top of her head
> and always said,
> "Todos los gringos se parecen."
> ("All Anglos look alike.")
or Tía Anita—always teaching,
> smart, proper, decent,
Tía Sara, Tía Eloisa, Tía Febe—
all in church, always in church.
Sofía said, "Well, I play
Tennessee Ernie Ford and Mahalia Jackson
on Sunday mornings."
And she *did*,
and sang along,
never learning that only singing in church
"counted."

She never made it through school either.
Instead of Polish jokes, the family told Sofía jokes:

"Remember that time at the lake, con Sofía?
      —Sophie! Come out of the water! It's raining!
      —No, me mojo! (I'll get wet!)
Always a little embarrassed
by her lack of wisdom,
lack of piety.

After she died, they didn't know what to say.
Didn't feel quite right saying
"She's always been a good Christian."
So they praised the way
"siempre se arreglaba la cara"
"se cuidaba"
and the way she never "fooled around"
even though she could've
after Uncle Raymond died
when she was still young
(Only 71).

A funeral comes every 2 years in the family now
just like the births did
60 to 80 years ago.
I remember a picture of a young flapper
with large eyes—Tía Sofía.
Between the tears,
we bump into the coffin by accident,
and get scared
and start laughing.
It seems appropriate.

It also seems appropriate
to sing
in a Black Tex-Mex
"Blueberry Hee-uhl."

Esa casa ya no existe

"Me siento muy cansado" dijo el viejito barbón, y cerró los ojos pa' sonar otra vez.

"Ta loco," decía la hija, "Todavía habla de ir pa' su país. ¿Y cómo vas a ir? ¿A pié?"

"A-a-a-ay, ya me voy pa' la casa, pa' ver a mis hermanas y a los compañeros que viven allí por mi calle. Y a ese cura condenao que me regañó. Y pa' sentarme en la plaza por un rato."

Y la hija se reía, "¿No te acuerdas, viejo? Ya se murieron todas tus hermanas. ¿Y cuál calle? Hace 70 años que te fuiste. Esa casa ya no existe." Y se salía del cuarto para attender a su que hacer.

Y el viejito todavía murmurando, "Sí me voy. Sí me voy a ir. Pero ahoritita no. Porque la vieja 'ta muy enfermita y no la puedo dejar al momento... ¿Vieja?... ¿Vieja, estás bien?...Vieja, ¡Contesta!"

Y el viejo comenzó a sentirse muy mal. Y el viejo se acordó.... "Pos ahora sí me voy. Ahora sí. Ya me voy. Ya me voy pa' mi casa."

Y la hija sacudía la cabeza, "No se le quita lo loco. Esa casa ya no existe." Pero el viejito se quedó con ganas de ir para su casa.

Un día el viejito paró de murmurar y de pelear. "Me siento muy cansado," dijo el viejito barbón y cerró los ojos para sonar otra vez. Y soñando de su casa, se fue para su casa.

Pos, sí, la viejita enfermita ya se fue. Y el viejito barbón también se fue. Y hasta la hija mandona también se ha muerto. Y la casucha de mis abuelos se cayó.

A veces me siento cansada de trabajar. A veces digo "Ya me voy pa' la casa." Y me siento a pensar, y me acuerdo...que esa casa ya no existe.

Los Corts 1. (la madre)

Las dos de la tarde y el calor.
Sudor pegajoso saliendo hasta de los ojos.
Cuando yo era chamacuela, me encantaban estas tardes
porque podía ir a buscar los gatos del barrio
dormiditos en sus rincones.
Pero ahora es mija la que les va a buscar
Sí, esos mismos gatos roñosos y flacos
Y yo que ya no puedo respirar
de tanto calor que hace en este cuartito.
Me acuerdo de cuando era muy bonita—
Ahora el cuerpo se me va desbaratando cada día
Y la cara se va cayendo, y cuando lo arreglo,
parece de plástico, o de payasa.
¿Ya qué soy? Sólo sudor y dolores.
Uju—el bebito ya se despertó.
Mañana tendré que ir al welfare.
…Las tres de la tarde y el calor.

Los Corts 2. (el chamaquito)

¡Jiiiii-jo! ¡Me jayé un daime!
¡Ta hueno eso!
Pa los airplanes que venden de wood
(¿O eran de cuara esas?)
Nuimporta—hasta los beisbol carts se compran a nicle
(También esos dientes de wax…)
Cuando llega Deri del trabajo, le voy a decir,
O le asusto con los dientes.
Y esa vieja mala a la tiendita
que siempre me tá regañando,
Le voy a enseñar ese daime
Pa que vea
Pa que *vea*…

Los Corts 3. (la pachuquita)

Oye tú—nomás no. La Silvia no vale nada.
Ta bien puta. Corriendo tras el Larry. Y él no la quiere.
Yo sé—porque me anda buscando a mí. He tol my brother.
Y después he asked me if I'd meet him a la tiendita afterschool.
Ta bien cool ese—ta pero *chulo*.
Es el más good-looking de to'a la class.
Hijo, y el otra día traiba esa camisa azulita
con el collar p'arriba así, y se veía su medallón en el chest,
y como siempre los zapatos shainados y el white hanky—
ta bien pa'cito!

Y La Silvia piensa que lo va agarrar
—pero nomás con cadenas, muchacha —
porque anda trás ésta aquí. Y yo no lo voy a correr.
Me dicen que she's gonna jump me,
pero tú no te apuras, manita—yo me defiendo.
Pinche puta, con la navaja se la entierro esas ideas.
Yo me defiendo. Porque nadie le insulta a La Dot.

Ey—la Mary Pester le taba escribiendo dirty notes
a La Silvia, y ella también patrás—
y taban diciendo malas cosas de Teodora. Me dijo Rosie.
Y que Manda y Rosie y la Teodora s'iban a juntar en P.E.
para dárselo a Pester y a Silvia.
¡You *bet*, muchacha! Aquí toy–lista!
Ajá, y a ver a quién más juntamos, porque La Silvia
se junta con todas esas gordonas feotas
que tan pero perras pa pelear.
Sí, en las showers, pa que no vea la Miss Hensley,
porque no le gusta que peleamos
en el gym floor.

Los Corts 4. (the dropout)

N'ombre, ya no voy.
Aunque 'buelita me diga.
Ese honroom teesher loco, pinche, caga'o
Ya no pue'e cerme *na'a.*
¡Porque yo no me dejo!
¿Y qué se creen?
Tan fufurrí y tan smart que se creen...
Yo no soy tonto.
Pero me ponen las *hardest* questions—
Yo *no soy* tonto
¿Y qué m'importa si *soy* tonto—
¡mejor que ser *loco!*
They don' *like* me, y siempre acusándome a mí.
N'ombre, ya no voy.
Aunque 'buelita me diga.
(And I *wasn't* spikking Spenish.
I *wasn't!!*)

Los Corts 5. (la viejita)

Sí, entre, entre.
Usted es la que trabaja con El Padre Rodríguez. Pos la casa es
humilde, pero es suya. Para servirle, Teófila Hernández de Soto.
Soto, ese fue mi esposo. Sí, el de ese retrato allá— Cuando
éramos jovencitos—reciéncasaditos—nomás teníamos el Benny
Chuniar y La Lupita. Uh—y la Lupita ya es grande—ya hasta
se casó su *hijo*. Ese es, sí, ese en el T.V.—cuando fue su gradu-
ey-chon de jaiskul. Y esa bebita a'i en la mesita es mi nieta la
más reciente, pero allí
nomás tenía los tres años, y ahora fíjate que ya tiene los siete.
Sí, tengo mucha familia—digo, de los hijos y los nietos—
porque ya de primos y de hermanos ya casi todos se han
muerto. De hijos y de hijas tengo muchos, y nunca me dejan
sola. Todos se han casado menos mijo el menor, Rudy (Rodolfo
le puse, como mi hermano.) Ese es, el que está de uniforme de
soldao. Sí, fue para Vietnam, y gracias a Dios, me lo mandaron
bueno y sano otra vez. Nomás que … me lo llevaron de muy
muchacho y muy simpatico y siempre sonriendo, y ahora a
veces se me pone medio-triste y se mete a pelear. Me dice que
es porque le hacen menos y le insultan. Y dice que a veces es
porque es mexicano. Y yo le digo que más antes fue peor, y que
su papa también tuvo que defenderse, ha sido así por mucho
tiempo, que no se enoje.
Pero no puede hallar trabajo
y, a veces, yo entiendo
y yo también me enojo,
pero nomás aquí adentro.
Aquí
adentrito,
y no le digo a nadien.

II. Spirits Between Siglos

Warning

Don't smell the smoke of a Brown ghost
who keeps starving White
and dying Brown.
He causes *mitotes* like a Texan Indian
and then goes through the Winter
sucking on cactus skins and searching
for overlooked mesquite beans
gone Brown.
Instead he finds Spanish missionaries too
eager to adore him and nations too
foreign to respect him, but only one
or two
mesquite beans.

Aquí

He wanders through the crooked streets
that mimic river beds Before
and breathes the anxious air in traffic
filled with tension left from wooded crossroads in attack
He shops the windows, happy,
where the stalking once was good
and his kitchen floor is built on bones
of venison once gently roasted.

"It's a good place for a party!" he concurs
to friends now dressed in jeans.

The ground was already beaten smooth
and festive by the joy of ancient dances.

He feels the warmth,
and doesn't know his soul is filled
with the spirit of coyotes past.

"Cuilmas"

snaking rhythms of peopled heat
   shuffle-shove through daylight's timeclocks
      stopping only seconds to sip air from
         the un-Angloed walls
            of some adobe, cedar-posted structure
               centuries too old for even urban
                  "Renewal" to destroy

              they rest
                 knowing that night's grace renewed
                  will bring them back the city's
                     Spanish soul
                       Indian goal
                         Mexican music
                           and the cool whisper of the
                           Chicano

                         "cuilmas…"

San Cuilmas is an old Chicano nickname for San Antonio, popularized with the Pachucos of the 1940's, and again with the Chicano Movement of the 60s and 70s.

Resfrío de alma

Rru-rru-rru
canta la abuela caridad
y te arregla el almohada
me acomoda la cobija
Pone un tecito a hervir
y espera el alivio.

¡Ajay!

A hearty laugh rumbles
and un grito mexicano—¡Ajay!

His eyes aglow like emerald embers
of unknown colors
sometimes light, sometimes dark,
always dreaming

Sinvergüenza smile dances in to say
"Qué raza tan más bonita"
while his brown hands turn problems slowly
into solutions

And his singing voice
refuses to know the meaning
of defeat.

Ancient House

In that tall-ceilinged ancient eight-walled house
where all my midnight dreams are born,
cuddled like children, fed *chocolate* in cups,
and taught to *amasar* tortillas
just like tía.

In that tall-ceilinged wooden-doored house
owned by cold drafts and toasted spaces
chuleando magic-flamed gas heaters
where my thoughts ae warmed
until they have enough *chiste* in them
to move.

In that tall-ceilinged solid-floored house
engraved with the secrets and scars
of five generations
and ten ideations
and a hundred inspirations
and the shapes and the colors and the corners
of my mind.

In that cold-windowed house
lies a woman
Old and silent with large roving eyes
Bare beneath her clothes in a shrunken frame,
and thin as onionskin over bones.

Her hand reaches out of a mattress.
and we discover
she is still
alive.

Her skin, worn so old it is almost translucent,
absorbs us
and her organs are visible and audible
like miracles
she fragile-ly
breathes.

In that tall-ceilinged house,
in that tall-ceilinged room
with too many walls and corners to count
she possesses us with her eyes in her breath,
her life in her death.

We try to move her
and her clothes fall aside, shedding petals,
and we stare at her too-naked old-woman's breasts
and are ashamed
for her helplessness.

Her eyes search us
reach like arms
dress themselves
and crawl out of the mattress.

We do not know what to say
with our sight
and her eyes begin to cover us
with hand-made healing quilts.
They stroke us with compassion
and they grow a shade in power.
They move and dance
and as I watch
I am absorbed.

I lean over the still body, still mattress-bound,
and wonder who she is
and why I care
so much.

In this tall-ceilinged ancient eight-walled house
owned by cold drafts and volcanic spaces
I breathe in through her onionskin lungs
and know,
with her eyes too old to need vision to see
that she
is
me.

Caminitos

The pathways of my thoughts are cobbled with
    mesquite blocks
        and narrow-winding,
    long and aged like the streets of
        san fernando de bexar
            y la villa real de san antonio

    pensive
        y callados
    cada uno con su chiste
        idiosyncracy
            crazy turns
    that are because they are,
        centuries magic

cada uno hecho así,
        y with a careful
            capricho touch,
                así.

They curl slowly into ripples,
    earthy and cool like the Río Medina
        under the trees
            silently singing, standing still,
    and flowing, becoming,
became
and always as always
    still fertile, laughing, loving,
        alivianada
        Río Medina
            under the trees,
                celebrating life.

They end up in the monte, chaparral,
   llenos de burrs, spurs
      pero libres
Running through the hills freefoot
   con aire azul
      blue breaths peacefully taken
         between each lope
            remembering venado
               remembering conejos
                  remembering
                     where
                        we came from

III. Cuentos Para El Curandero

Quality Literature

-Dr. Dumont?- said a quiet voice from the back row of the World Lit class, as the bell rang and the distinguished professor collected his papers to dash from the room.

-Yes?- said Dumont in his crisp pseudo-British accent, as a hazy face with a name he didn't remember approached him.

-You said the other day, that, uh, we could write our critique-thing on any author, just to get it approved by you first, and I, well, I was in the library the other day, and they got this real good book by Elena Martínez called *La Tierra Grita*, and I wanna do mine on that.

-Elena Martínez? I don't recall the name—is she the poetess from Chile?

-No, sir. She's a Chicana, and it's about a campesino family in—

-It's Chicano Literature? No, I'm afraid I just can't approve that. Read it if you wish, but for your report we need quality literature, and Chicano literature simply isn't *quality*.

-But this stuff's good! I mean, it's the first stuff I ever seen that really talks about real things. There's writers like Toribio Salinas, and—have you read Juan Rivera, sir?

-No but why don't you look into Samuel Beckett's *En Attendant Godot*? The French existentialist theatre is really superb in its handling of the alienation of the individual in society. The profundity and subtlety in its absurd context magnify the impact of its universal reality. It speaks to the commonest of situations, and yet elevates to the philosophically sublime the lowest of human positions. I would think it would be an excellent topic for you.

-But have you read Inéz de León, sir?

-No, but I really think Beckett's French existentialist theatre would provide an almost unlimited opportunity for development and commentary. There are some books that might interest you on it—now there's one by Fontaine on the peculiar juxtaposition of characters in *Godot,* and there's quite a few references available on the manneristic existentialism evident in Beckett's theatre. I'm certain our library would have quite a good bit on it and—

-Well how about Frank Sanchez? Have you read him?

-No, but there simply hasn't *been* any quality Chicano literature. If you *must* have something in Spanish, try Darío or Bor-hays or Cervantes. Darío has been highly acclaimed in Madrid, and even Paris- said the professor, examining with slight curiosity the face of the student who he now faintly recalled as having made very poor marks on the last exam. "Of course," he thought.

-Soledad Cantú has been published in Spain. Could I write on her? Sir?

Dumont continued to shake his head, gathered his papers under his arm, leaned into the face of the student, and stated emphatically, "But it hasn't even been critiqued in the PMLA! And *until* it's critiqued in the PMLA, I *can't* say it's quality literature!"

And the professor walked off into a semi-colon...as the face of the student became an epic poem.

And When I Dream Dreams...

when I dream dreams,
I dream of *YOU*
Rhodes Jr. School
and the lockers of our minds
that were always jammed stuck
or that always hung open
and would never close,
no matter *how* hard You tried,
we messed up the looks of the place
and wouldn't be neat and organized
and look like we were s'posed to look
and lock like we were s'posed
to lock.

yea that's right
I dream of *you*
degrees later
and from both sides of the desk
my dreams take place
in your two-way halls,
Hall Guards from among us,
human traffic markers,
bumps on the road
between the lanes,
to say, when we were s'posed to say,
where to turn left, where right,
and how to get where you were going—
"You'll never get to high school
speakin' Spanish," I was told
Nice of them, they thought, to not report me,
breakin' state law, school law, speakin' dirty
(speakin' Spanish)

and our tongues couldn't lump it
and do what they were s'posed to do.
So instead I reminded others
to button buttons
and tuck shirttails in.

I never graduated to a
Cafeteria Guard,
who knows how they were picked.
We thought it had something to do
with the FBI
or maybe the Principal's office.
So we got frisked
Boys in one line
Girls in another
twice every day
entering lunch and leaving
Check—no knives on the boys
Check—no dangerous weapons on the girls
(like mirrors,
perfume bottles,
deodorant bottles,
or teased hair.)
So we wandered the halls
cool chuca style
"no se sale"
and unawares
never knowing
other junior highs were never frisked
never knowing
what the teachers said in the teachers lounge
never knowing we were (s'posed to be)
the toughest junior high in town.
And the lockers of our minds
are now assigned to other minds,

carry other books,
follow other rules,
silence other tongues,
go to other schools—
Schools of Viet Nam,
Schools of cheap cafe,
Schools of dropout droppings, prison pains, and
cop car's bulleted brains.

Marcelino thought the only way
to finance college
was the Air Force
(G.I. Bill and *good pay!*)
War looked easy
compared to here
Took his chances on a college education,
Took his pay on a shot-down helicopter
in a brown-skinned 'Nam,
with a pledge of allegiance in his mind
he had memorized through Spanish-speaking teeth.
As a Hall Guard, he was "clean-cut"
Now—cut clean down
in a hospital ward,
paralyzed below the lips,
that still speak Spanish
slowly.
Silvia thought no one had the right
to tell her what to do.
One year out of junior high, she bitterly bore
her second pregnancy,
stabbed forks onto cafe tables
and slushed coffee through the crowds
sixteen hours a day, and she was *fifteen*
and still fighting to say
"I HAVE A RIGHT TO BE *ME!*"

And Lalo with a mind that could write in his sleep
growing epics from eyes that could dream
now writes only the same story
over and over
until the day
that it's *all*
over,
as he's frisked and he's frisked and he's frisked
and they keep finding
nothing
and even when he's *out*
his mind is always *in*
prison.

Like Lupe's mind
that peels potatoes
and chops *repollo*
and wishes its boredom was less
than the ants in the hill
and never learned to read because
the words were in English
and she
was in Spanish.

I wonder what we would *do*,
Rhodes Junior School,
if we had all those
emblems of *you*
stamped on our lives
with a big Red *"R"*
like the letter sweaters
we could never
afford
to buy.

I keep my honorary
junior school diploma
from you
right next to the B.A., M.A.,
etcetera to a Ph.D.
because it means
I graduated
from you
and when I dream dreams,
—how I wish my dreams
had graduated too.

P
E
O
Z
R
B
O
I
L

Torn-up billboards wave goodbye
with their shreds in the wind
Rio Grande City has one stoplight
Isn't that enough?
An empire alone
full of proud emperors and empresses
Each ruling their domain, their tecorucho, their handplow
The birds warn on the way in – the moat of rabbits, turtles, snakes,
a winding road, coyotes, lechuzas keep out the outside world
"Y por qué hay discriminación contra el mexicano?" me preguntan.
A centuries-old world full of mexicanos pelirrojos,
Blondes, morenos, y ojos borrados.
Todos vienen de Rio Grande City.
O de La Grulla.
Fort Ringgold was here once.
The soldiers se cansaron
because there was nothing here to fight.
The defense of the Rio Grandeanos is complete.
La tierra, el cielo, el sol los protege

photography and big cities But always came
back to take his best photographs in RioGrandeCity.
  ¿Lo conoces? le pregunto al señor.
    "Era mi sobrino . . . Hace un Año
      que desapareció. La última carta
        la recibió su abuela, 'taba pensando
          de ir a meditar alguna parte
RioGrandeanos   callada." You see
                          what happens to
magic valley   whostaytoolong
                          away from the
vanish   They lose their
        into thin air   glue and

                survive allá
                criado en el   atom by atom
                deRioGrandeCity Es dificil
survive   cuando se han
                                 pozo perdido
sus   Es dificil

                            sin
          coyotes brujos
          que los protegen.
          Aquí el aire es diferente
          Y no se puede
              comprar.

Voyage

I was the fourth ship.
     Behind Niña, Pinta, Santa María,
     Lost at sea while watching a seagull,
     Following the wind and sunset skies,
     While the others set their charts.

I was the fourth ship.
     Breathing in salt and flying with clouds,
     Sailing moonbreezes and starvision nights,
     Rolling into the wave and savoring its lull,
     While the others pointed their prows.

I was the fourth ship.
     Playfully in love with the sea,
     Eternally entwined with the sky,
     Forever vowed to my voyage,
     While the others shouted "Land."

IV. Un Tecito

Medicine Poem

Sickness lies around us like rotting feelings
  splintering minds on the spears of a bored and angry crowd
  and splattering the faces of children with blood

Sickness robs bandages to pay bombs
  and build better rockets, and better than those better
  in a winning-game that never wins

Sickness nabs young black children playing in Atlanta
  and lays their empty bodies, laughingly, by the road
  to match the brown notches in policemen's guns

Sickness leaves health hiding in a grass-roofed shack
  in a Kickapoo Indian Village
  under the international bridge
  that holds Eagle Pass, Texas
  to Piedras Negras, Mexico
  where native peoples between two foreign nations
  use dual citizenship
  to ward off dual dangers.
  And health huddles, hides, in healing huts of cardboard
      and grass,
  never knowing which way to go to escape the madness

Our hurting, healing must run in the right direction
  and swiftly, with quick glances back,
  carrying with it always the medicine pouch, intact
      with human bonding.

Must run, must heal, must leave behind
for wars
and poems
must always
have an end.

Curandera

Afuera de tu casa,
   entre la hierba buena y el anís
   estoy planteada.

    Vine aquí a verte,
  a preguntar tus ojos tierra-grises
    a escuchar a tu voz mesquite seco
      a observar tus manos sabi-siglos
        a llevarme alguna hierba de una de tus botellas.

        The smell of her kitchen and the sound
           of her chanclas
        are almost within my sight. Her wisdom,
        the secrets that age has let grow
        slowly
        in her window
        like a wild coffee-can-seeded plant
        of no name
        of no dignity or fuss
        beyond that
        of its own
        presence.

        Those aged clouded eyes have seen the
           bodies of the dead
        sink below the crust of red-dirt sand
        and felt the swelling stomach's gift
        emerge a blood-red man.

        Observing, sinking in thoughts,
        I have gone no further.

At a distance that will not stand still.
My feet stuck, rooting

The gnarled and earthing fingers of her mind
    feel the current in my veins
        and see the twilit shapes within my bodycaverns

Curandera,
    te siento arrastrando tus chanclas
        por los arcos-portales de mis venas,
    bajando los botes de tu sabiduría
        del gabinete de mi cabeza.

        El perro aulla, el rocío me resfría,
        mis pies cementados en sus huellas,
        mis ojos mudos preguntando la luz de tu ventana.
        Tiemblo aquí en tu jardín,
        entre la hierba buena y el anís.

-El orno es terremoto dormido...

En tus ollitas hierben ya

        las hojas

            de mis sueños.

Tierra Brujo

perceptions rebel, enchant the
   spiraled lizards of reality
      del desierto wilderness
      de mi *terra incognita,*
        wild country undefined
           avoided by the civilized
           worshipped by adventurers

   ojos de iguana cross borders, make them disappear
   esqueleto de arco iris glows, rainbow in a drought
   noche prowls through aullido's echo
      crawls into the sun-brittled day
      dares the undaunted
      dissects the insincere

Tierra Brujo, cactus cuna,
   defying comfort, you broke
   your milkteeth on montañas
   nursed yourself on sudor
   defying gender, survived

Tierra Brujo
   Tierra Brujo
      por más que han tratado
      nunca te han conquistado.

Rain Seeds

rain seeds
like drops of cool beginning
kiss earth in soft silence
and treasure-cradle
hidden underneath the grass
their secret song, sweet-whispered, saved
Like drops of hope from my parched lips,
they study each slow unborn sun
and await the time
                    to sprout

Y cuando pienso en tí

y cuando pienso en tí...

pienso en las olas de mares secretos
que jamás han conocido ni mentiras ni dominación
que broncas nacen y broncos bailan
y broncas viven su exaltación.

pienso en las rocas bruñidas, alisadas,
esculpidas por los siglos con la marca de amor,
de la pared más alta del castillo más viejo
en el valle lozano de mi corazón.

pienso en las jarras enterradas, vidriadas,
que, sencillas, sobreviven dueño, duelo, y civilización,
que en su obra, dan vida, y en su vida, dan gracia,
que refrescan, y cargan agua, cuento, y canción.

pienso en tus ojos, antorchas encendidas,
que regalan miradas, caminos, y calor.
pienso en planetas de lunas gemelas
de tierras perladas de raro valor.
de seres valientes de ojos danzantes
que sueñan y cambian su gema color.

pienso en tu alma de calor y coraje
ardor y justicia, viveza y amor.
pienso en cristales de eterna pureza,
diamantes ardientes de espontánea belleza
adornando cavernas de primordial creación
adornando el universo con su paz y pasión.

pienso en lo siempre de un manantial
brotando melodías y gozo y frenesí.
pienso en un viento de vida-aire sinigual
y en un eterno querer cuando pienso en tí.
un eterno querer, cuando pienso en tí.

Author's Note, 2012

It was a different time, a different world, but one hungry and hurting for truth, for compassion, for healing.

These poems and pieces of short fiction, written between 1975 and 1979, and published together in 1983, represent a part of that search and that Movimiento of awakening and protest, critical theory and creative cultural affirmation. It was also a world of hope, in which a poem or a short piece of fiction might reach someone, change something, spark a new analysis, open a door or a mind. It is my belief that they did. Many of these poems also went on to travel other paths after this book. "Voyage" was published in half a dozen high school and college literature textbooks, and became a poster on the city buses of Austin. "And When I Dream Dreams" became the inspiration for an award-winning, student-made documentary film of the same name. "Tía Sofía" was included in the audio series, *A Century of Recorded Poetry*, and was also featured in an audio exhibit at the National Women's Museum. The five voices in "Los Corts" were performed throughout Europe, New Zealand and the Americas. Thelma Muraida's stunning illustrations captured perfectly the spirit of the text, and were exhibited at the San Antonio Public Library. It was the book *Curandera* that caused Alex Haley to seek me out and relate how it reverbrated with the voices of Africaniste poets. For years, it was used in Tucson Unified School District's exemplary Mexican American Studies Curriculum, and in other classrooms throughout the Southwest.

But it was not until 2012 that the book was banned. Just as Wings Press was preparing to release this volume in 30th anniversary edition, the state administration of Arizona banned the teaching of ethnic studies in public schools, and numerous significant books were removed from Mexican American Studies Classrooms at Tucson Unified School District. Paolo

Tafolla performing in the Zach Scott Theater (Austin, Texas, 1978),
with Gloria Partida and Leticia Galindo.

Freire's *Pedagogy of the Oppressed*, Arturo Rosales' *Chicano! The History of the Mexican Civil Rights Movement*, Sandra Cisneros' *House on Mango Street*, Shakespeare's *The Tempest*, and dozens of others, including *Curandera*, were all suspect and not to be taught in the context of Mexican American culture. The message was clear. Teaching students to be proud of Mexican-American or Indigenous culture is a sin. Celebrating or even recognizing the experience or history or voices of these peoples is against the law.

Yes, we live in a different world from the one in which *Curandera* was originally published. Thirty years later, accomplishments we never would have imagined have happened. Events we never could have dreamed have filled the calendar dates, and gone into history. The surprising thing, though, is that new insults we never would have predicted have been spit out, filled with hate and prejudice. Echoes of educational mistakes repeated through the centuries have been repeated again. Oppressions, repressions, suppressions of a people have continued, often unchanged. We have made giant steps forward and, sometimes, monstrous steps backward.

We find ourselves more experienced, more accomplished, more astute, but somehow just as hungry and hurting for truth, for compassion, for healing, and every bit as much, in need of a curandera. Here she is, still. Offering her lessons from the hearts of our homes; arranging safe underground railroad passage to the spirits between the siglos; teaching a thing or two to even the most experienced of our curanderos, leaving them surprised and speechless; and preparing for us a tecito, a steaming cup of cinnamon tea to warm us, envelop us, heal us, and open our understanding to see through ojos sanos, eyes filled with truth, compassion and love.

Gracias, curandera spirit, you don't know how badly our world still needs you.

Carmen Tafolla
San Antonio, Tejas
January 30, 2012

Acknowledgments (1983)

This book would not have been possible without the loving help of Moisés and Angela. Deepest thanks to: Angela de Hoyos, for the inspired coordination, the mata de canela, and the unswerving encouragement; Moisés Sandoval for the layout, design, and typesetting of this book; Rolando Hinojosa, whose literary works have set a new standard of quality and resonance for this continent; Thelma Ortíz Muraida, for the cover design and illustrations whose visual soul and spirit transcend the paper; Rose Mary Tafolla, for the photograph and the faith; Doña María Ortíz, por su inspiración casera; and to Dr. Ernesto M. Bernal, for his supportiveness and appreciation of creativity, curanderismo, and me.

También, gratitud espiritual a las abuelas—Josefina Moreno Duarte, quien tenía la mano curandera; María Gonzales Marroquín, quien herbía el tecito; Eloisa Sánchez de Tafolla, quien crecía las matas y hierbitas; y María Martínez de Bernal, quien daba la bendición; a mis padres—María y Mariano Tafolla, y Linda y Ernesto Bernal; a Ann, a Sean, a Cielos Tafolla Bernal, y a los que vendrán; a mi "baby brother"; a mi Hermana, a mis parientes, colegas, amigos, enemigos, y estrangeros. A Dios, por su creación.

Acknowledgments (2012)

To all of those above, still. Even especially, now. After thirty years of support and faith from family and friends, the important treasures of a life committed to healing the alma become even clearer. And I am grateful to you ALL, tesoritos.

Los que vendrán ya han venido- Mari, Israel, Ariana. Y de los que estaban, algunos se han ido – Mariano Tafolla, Linda y Ernesto Martínez Bernal, mi hermana Eloisa, y la linda madrina de este libro, Angela de Hoyos. Pero están ausentes nomás en cuerpo; presentes en mis días quedarán. And others have joined in, woven into this ejército del alma, united in fierce commitment and a rock hard hope for the future: Norma Elia Cantú, Oralia Garza de Cortez, Celina Marroquín, Janka Klescova, Velma Nanka-Bruce, Mariana Aitches, Bryce Milligan, David Hernández, all those who love books, and los Librotraficantes and their caravan of banned books, who will carry this book to where the healing is most needed. Gracias, again, and always.

About the Author

Carmen Tafolla is a native of the West-Side barrios of San Antonio and the author of more than 20 books. Tafolla has been recognized by the National Association for Chicano Studies for work which "gives voice to the peoples and cultures of this land" and has received numerous recognitions, including: the Art of Peace Award for work which contributes to peace, justice, and human understanding; the Charlotte Zolotow Award for best children's picture book writing; the Americas

Tafolla reading at the Elisabet Ney Museum (Austin, Texas, 1980).

Award, presented at the Library of Congress; two Tomas Rivera Book Awards; two ALA Notable Books; and two international Latino Book Awards. A member of the Texas Institute of Letters, she is currently Writer-in-Residence for Children's, Youth & Transformative Literature at the University of Texas San Antonio.

Tafolla received her Ph.D. in Bilingual Education from the University of Texas in 1982 and is still doing postgraduate work on her Ph.C. (Curandera of Philosophy.) She lives in San Antonio, Texas with her husband, Dr. Ernesto M. Bernal, her daughter Ariana, her 94-year-old mother, three cats, two computers, one typewriter, a house full of books, a yard full of hierbitas, many dreams, some remedios, and a molcajete.

About the Artist

Thelma Ortíz Muraida is an accomplished artist and graphic designer from San Antonio, Texas. She has designed numerous book covers, illustrated articles for national publications and journals, and illustrated two children's books. She also created the cover art and design for five of Carmen Tafolla's books. Muraida received her Bachelor of Arts from Trinity University, and continued her training with graduate work at Eastern Michigan University and the Art Student's League in New York.

Thelma Ortíz Muraida, ca. 1980

Colophon

This 30th anniversary edition of *Curandera,* by Carmen Tafolla, has been printed on 70 pound "natural" paper containing a percentage of recycled fiber. Titles have been set in Cochin type, the text in Adobe Caslon type. All Wings Press books are designed and produced by Bryce Milligan.

On-line catalogue and ordering
available at
www.wingspress.com

Wings Press titles are distributed
to the trade by the
Independent Publishers Group
www.ipgbook.com
and in Europe by
www.gazellebookservices.co.uk

Available as an ebook.